What It Means

Based on On Being Different by Merle Miller

James Corley

methuen | drama

LONDON • NEW YORK • OXFORD • NEW DELHI • SYDNEY

METHUEN DRAMA
Bloomsbury Publishing Plc
50 Bedford Square, London, WC1B 3DP, UK
1385 Broadway, New York, NY 10018, USA
29 Earlsfort Terrace, Dublin 2, Ireland

BLOOMSBURY, METHUEN DRAMA and the Methuen
Drama logo are trademarks of Bloomsbury Publishing Plc

First published in Great Britain 2023

Cover artwork by Steph Pyne

Cover photograph by Cam Harle

A catalogue record for this book is available from the British Library.

A catalog record for this book is available from the Library of Congress.

ISBN: PB: 978-1-3504-2516-3
ePDF: 978-1-3504-2517-0
eBook: 978-1-3504-2518-7

Series: Modern Plays

Typeset by Mark Heslington Ltd, Scarborough, North Yorkshire

To find out more about our authors and books visit
www.bloomsbury.com and sign up for our newsletters.

Nisha Oza for The Lot Productions presents

WHAT IT MEANS

by James Corley

Based on *On Being Different* by Merle Miller

What It Means was first performed at Wilton's Music Hall
on Wednesday 4 October 2023.

CAST

Richard Cant – Merle Miller

Cayvan Coates – Boy from Pittsburgh

CREATIVE TEAM

Director – Harry Mackrill

Writer – James Corley

Producer – Nisha Oza

Set/Costume Designer – Justin Arienti

Lighting Designer – Martha Godfrey

Sound Designer – Beth Duke

Creative Associate – Ayesha Antoine

PRODUCTION TEAM

Production Manager – Anthony Newton

Company Stage Manager – Lorna Seymour

Assistant Stage Manager – Zeena Avari

The Lot Productions would like to thank the following individuals and organisations for their generous support: Doulla Croft, David Hare, Nick Hytner, Jonathan Kent, Jonathan Levy, Kate Fahy, Diana & Peter Murray, Olivia and Robert Temple, Melanie J. Johnson, Kenny Wax, Eleanor Lloyd Productions, Trafalgar Entertainment and Wessex Grove

We wish to acknowledge financial support from Stage One, a registered charity that invests in new commercial productions. Stage One supports new UK theatre producers and productions, and is committed to securing the future of commercial theatre through educational and investment schemes.

Special thanks to Carol Hanley for trusting us with Merle's story.

Richard Cant – Merle Miller

Richard Cant is a stage and screen actor who has most recently starred in: *The Vortex* (Chichester Festival Theatre); *Orlando* (Garrick Theatre); *The Normal Heart* (National Theatre); *Wife* (Kiln Theatre); *Henry VI: Rebellion*, *Wars of the Roses*, *Maydays* (RSC).

Other theatre includes: *Mr Gum and the Dancing Bear*, *War Horse* (National Theatre); *Talent* (Sheffield Crucible Theatre); *After Edward*, *Edward II* (Sam Wanamaker Playhouse); *My Night with Reg*, *Saint Joan* (Donmar Warehouse); *Medea* (Almeida Theatre); *The Trial* (Young Vic); *Stella* (LIFT).

TV includes: *It's a Sin*, *The Crown*, *Taboo*, *Silent Witness*, *Outlander*, *Mapp and Lucia*, *Vexed*, *Above Suspicion*, *Gunpowder, Treason & Plot*, *Doctor Who*, *Bleak House*, *Shackleton*, *Midsomer Murders* and *The Way We Live Now*.

Film includes: *My Policeman*, *Mary Queen of Scots*, *Stan and Ollie*, *Take Care*, *Sparkle* and *The Lawless Heart*.

Cayvan Coates – Boy from Pittsburgh

Cayvan Coates graduated from RADA in 2019.

Television credits include: *Casualty* (BBC); *Midsomer Murders* (ITV); *Masters of the Air* (Apple TV+); *The Chelsea Detective* (Acorn); *Vera* (ITV).

Theatre credits include: *The Curious Incident of the Dog in the Night-time* (National Theatre).

Workshop credits include: *Fence* (Finborough Theatre); *Keep a Light on for Those Who Are Lost* (Bush Theatre).

Harry Mackrill (Director)

Harry Mackrill was Associate Director of Kiln Theatre 2018–19, and Resident Director of the Tricycle Theatre 2013–15. He trained as an actor at the Royal Welsh College of Music & Drama.

Theatre includes: *World's End*, *Boy with Beer* (King's Head Theatre); *Let Kilburn Shake* (Kiln Theatre).

Film includes: *Led by the Child* (The Lot); *Adjustments* (The Lot/If Opera); *Amber* (Synergy Theatre Project).

As Associate Director: *Angels in America*, *Peter Gynt*, *The Motherfucker with the Hat* (National Theatre); *Handbagged* (Tricycle Theatre, West End, UK tour, Washington); *Slaves of Solitude* (Hampstead Theatre).

Harry teaches acting and playwriting for Synergy Theatre Project, Mountview Academy of Theatre Arts and Islington Centre for Refugees & Migrants.

James Corley (Writer)

James Corley is a playwright, screenwriter and filmmaker. He grew up in East Anglia before moving to London to study acting at LAMDA. His first play, *World's End*, closed the King's Head Theatre's Queer Season in 2019 and was voted Theatre Weekly's No. 1 Best Off West End Production of the year. His award-winning short film *The Scene* premiered at the BFI Flare LGBTQI festival 2020 and was shortlisted for the Iris Prize Best British Short 2020. He has recently finished his third short, *Bone by Bone.*

Other written work includes *Twenty-Eight: Stories from the Section 28 Generation.*

James also teaches playwriting and acting for adults with autism at Community Focus in North London, and is a BAFTA Connect member.

Nisha Oza (Producer)

Nisha Oza began her career as part of the original National Theatre Live team, and has since worked across the subsidised and commercial sectors for organisations including the Royal Court Theatre, the Bridge Theatre, Kiln Theatre, Tamasha Theatre Company and National Theatre Productions.

Credits include Theatre Weekly's No. 1 Off-West End Production 2019 *World's End* by James Corley and the Iris Prize Best British Short Film nominee *The Scene*. As an independent producer, Nisha has worked with artists including Barney Norris, Polly Teale and Diyan Zora. She works as Development Manager for Synergy Theatre Project.

Nisha worked on the National Theatre's 50th Anniversary Broadcast, BBC Film's *London Road*, and as Project Manager for the National Theatre's Immersive Storytelling Studio.

She is a trustee for Stage One producers' charity and a MGFutures Bursary Recipient.

Justin Arienti (Set/Costume Designer)

Justin Arienti is a stage and costume designer who trained at the Accademia di Belle Arti di Brea in Milan and worked for the Atelier Carlo Colla & Figli worldwide before moving to London where he has been associate designer to Richard Hudson and other leading designers.

He designed the world premieres of the operas *La Tragédie de Carmen* Italian adaptation for *Operaoggi*; *Cyberiada* for the Wielki Theatre Poznan/Warsaw; *Maria di Venosa* at the Festival di MartinaFranca; and the ballets *Carmen* and *Romeo & Juliette* for François Mauduit Dance Company.

He has been the recipient of the Jan Kiepura Theatre Award for Best Design for the opera *Cyberiada* directed by Ran Arthur Braun. The same team received the award in the category Best Opera for the double bill *L'Enfant et Les Sortileges/Le Rossignol* also produced by the Wielki Theatre, Poznan.

Justin is a recurring designer on the BBC One flagship show *EastEnders*.

Martha Godfrey (Lighting Designer)

Martha Godfrey is a lighting and projection designer working across theatre, dance, musicals and live art. Past work includes: *The Invicibles* (Queen's Theatre Hornchurch); *Sugar Coat* (Southwark Playhouse); *Flies* (Shoreditch Town Hall); *Much Ado (The Remix)* (NYT, Duke of York Theatre); *The Prince* (Southwark Playhouse); *Mapping Gender* (tour & The Place); *Bangers* (tour & Soho Theatre); *But I'm a Cheerleader* (Turbine Theatre); *Passion Fruit* (New Diorama Theatre); *Home, I'm Darling* (Theatre Royal Bury St Edmunds); *Oliver Twist!* (Chester Storyhouse); *What Do You See* (Shoreditch Town Hall); *Redemption* (The Big House); *Pink Lemonade* (Bush Theatre); *Concrete Jungle Book* (Pleasance Theatre); *Fever Pitch* (Hope Theatre); *Around the World in Eighty Days* (Theatre Royal Bury St Edmunds); *Time and Tide* (Park Theatre); *Before I Was a Bear* (The Bunker); *I Wanna Be Yours* (UK tour and Bush Theatre); *Unknown Rivers* (Hampstead Theatre Downstairs); *We Dig* (Ovalhouse); *Cabildo* (Arcola Theatre); *GREY* (Ovalhouse); *WHITE* (Ovalhouse, Pleasance Edinburgh Fringe, UK tour); *Exceptional Promise* (Bush Theatre); *Fuck You Pay Me* (The Bunker/Rich Mix/ Assembly Rooms, Edinburgh Fringe/Vaults Festival).

Beth Duke (Sound Designer)

Beth Duke is a sound designer whose credits include: *Retrograde* (Kiln Theatre); *The Suspicions of Mr Whicher* (Watermill Theatre); *Strategic Love Play* (Belgrade Theatre/UK tour); *Infamous* (Jermyn Street Theatre); *The Trial of Josie K* (Unicorn Theatre); *Akedah* (Hampstead Theatre); *Beauty and the Beast* (Mercury Theatre); *Amma VR Experience* (Tara Theatre); *Death Drop: Back in the Habit* (Garrick Theatre/UK tour); *A Single Man* (Park Theatre); *Alice in Wonderland* (Mercury Theatre); *The Importance of Being Earnest* (English touring Theatre); *Bridgerton* (Secret Cinema); *Mad House* (Ambassadors Theatre); *Mog the Forgetful Cat* (Royal Derngate and Old Vic); *Robin Hood* (Bristol Old Vic); *Death Drop* (Garrick Theatre, Criterion Theatre and UK tour); *J'Ouvert* (Harold Pinter Theatre & BBC); *One Jewish Boy* (Trafalgar Studios, West End & UK tour); *Typical Girls* (Sheffield Crucible Theatre); *Scenes with Girls*, *Living Newspaper* (Royal Court Theatre).

Ayesha Antoine (Creative Associate)

Ayesha Antoine is an actor and playwright. She is currently adapting Sam Selvon's *The Housing Lark* into a calypso opera for The Lot Productions, as part of their ADAPT season.

Her theatre credits include: *White Teeth*, *The Wolf in Snakeskin Shoes*, *The House that Will Not Stand* (Kiln Theatre); *Out West* (Lyric Hammersmith); *The Suicide* (National Theatre); *Red Velvet*, *Dirty Great Love Story* (West End); *Hamlet* (Kenneth Branagh Company) .

Ayesha has been nominated for a Drama Desk Award and won the UK Theatre Award for Best Supporting Actress.

The History

September 1970. *Harper's Magazine* publish the article 'Homo/Hetero: The Struggle for Sexual Identity' in which Joseph Epstein states: 'If I had the power to do so, I would wish homosexuality off the face of the earth.'

The Gay Activists Alliance stage a sit-in at the Harper's office. But there are many ways to protest.

In his Glass House, hidden in the woods outside Brewster, New York, the acclaimed journalist and former editor of *Harper's Magazine* Merle Miller sits at his desk and begins to write.

September 1971. Merle, aged fifty-one, comes out in the *The New York Times Magazine*. The article in question, 'What It Means to Be a Homosexual', was a public declaration of identity, a rallying cry for equality and – ultimately – part of the fabric of protest that formed the modern LGBTQ+ movement.

Described as 'the most widely read and discussed essay of the decade', the article was published by Penguin as 'On Being Different' – one of the earliest memoirs to affirm the importance of coming out.

About Merle Miller

Merle Miller was born in a small town in Iowa in 1919 and attended the University of Iowa and London School of Economics. Miller was awarded two Bronze Stars for bravery during World War Two, both of which he later returned out of protest for American action in Vietnam. He was editor of *Harper's Magazine* and *Time* and was a contributing editor for *The Nation*. His books include the best-selling novels *That Winter* (1948) and *A Gay and Melancholic Sound* (1962), a comic non-fiction narrative about writing for television called *Only You, Dick Daring!* (1964) and several best-selling presidential biographies.

In 1971 'What It Means to be a Homosexual' made Miller one of the first prominent Americans to come out publicly. He died in 1986.

Why Merle, Why Now?

Sometimes I have to remind myself which words belong to *On Being Different*, Merle Miller's 1971 essay, and which to *What It Means*, the play adapted by James Corley.

I was sure that I could attribute 'silence is a habit' to Merle, only to be told they were written by James. This line is, for me, central to the play. It confirms that within a play about the power of words, the subtext is one of silence.

The Silent Generation is the term given to those born 1927 to 1945. Often known as the 'Traditionalists', they were also the generation that produced the leaders of the Civil Rights Movements and the voices behind 1960s counterculture.

Although born seven years earlier in 1920, much of Merle's life was characterised by this juxtaposition of silence and protest. As a writer, Merle knew the power of words and the importance of speaking up.

Only later, as described in *On Being Different*, did he learn the value of protest.

The balance between silence and protest has remained an important part of the fabric of Queer existence for the past fifty years. ACT UP, the grassroots activists who have fought for direct action to end AIDS since 1987, knew the danger of silence. The slogan SILENCE = DEATH exposed the truth behind international governmental responses to the epidemic.

I didn't know about ACT UP or Merle, or that I could belong to a Queer community, until my early twenties. I grew up shrouded in the silence created by Thatcher's Section 28. This silence led me, like Merle, to believe that I was the only one. The answer to me seemed entirely obvious: keep quiet.

I managed to maintain my silence until my mid-20s. Upon coming out I was greeted by the cocophany of Queer voices who had always been there – I just hadn't heard them yet. One of those voices was Merle Miller.

In 2010, I stood in Foyles Bookshop and read *On Being Different*. That day, I discovered part of myself for the first time – in words forty years old, written by someone born ninety years earlier on the other side of the world. Merle perfectly described my experience growing up in a world of silence. He was the first person to show me that there was a life waiting for me because of, not in spite of, the challenges I might have faced. A life that could be full of love and friendship and community – entirely whole.

For the last decade, *On Being Different* has guided me on my journey.

It took Merle courage to write his essay, to stand up and be counted. This courage enabled me, and thousands of others over the last fifty years, to accept themselves and be counted as part of a community. To end their own silence.

I wanted to make Merle's essay into a play so that these words could be spoken out loud again – in real time and space – and be heard as a collective experience by a contemporary audience.

In his adaptation, James has – like Merle – interwoven the names of pioneers from across the Queer community who stood up and shouted loudly for equality. Who ended the silence for so many.

Names like Kate Millett, Marcia P. Johnson, E.M. Forster.

This production is for them, and Merle, and all those voices who were here before us.

Harry Mackrill (Director)

PRODUCTIONS

About The Lot Productions

Nisha Oza (Creative Producer) and Harry Mackrill (Creative Director) met working as Producing Assistant and Resident Director at the Tricycle Theatre in 2016. After bonding over the experience of queueing for tickets to *Othello* at the Donmar Warehouse in 2008, they realised they were driven by the power of theatre in a similar way.

In 2020, the pandemic afforded the pair time to develop their vision for The Lot Productions and establish their working ethos as independent producing with an inclusive mindset.

Through support from Stage One, Arts Council England and MGCfutures, Nisha and Harry were able to secure the rights to three prominent texts and commission James Corley and Ayesha Antoine to write the first slate of work for The Lot.

What It Means will be followed by adaptations of *Burnt Sugar* by Avni Doshi and *The Housing Lark* by Sam Selvon, alongside the release of the short film *Led by the Child*.

thelotproductions.com | Twitter @thelotprods | Insta @thelotprods

QWAH x The Lot

Queer was always here

Queer Was Always Here began with two dinosaurs on a t-shirt. They were orange, they were gay, and they were in love – in a time before humans invented homophobia. That simple image of queer joy resonated more than we could have imagined. Soon, people were painting the dinos onto phone cases and tote bags, sculpting them, baking them into biscuits, and even getting them tattooed.

From that small beginning, we've grown into an organisation dedicated to celebrating queer joy, queer art, and queer history, whilst working in partnership with Choose Love to secure futures for LGBTQIA+ refugees and displaced people around the world.

Over the past year, we've raised more than £250,000 for a range of grassroots organisations providing essential support to vulnerable queer people fleeing conflict and persecution. With our help, over 900 people from Afghanistan to Ukraine have received direct assistance in the form of resettlement, legal aid, cash and food support, language programs, and more.

Queerness is much older than bigotry. From the animal kingdom to the non-binary priests of Ancient Mesopotamia, from Han Dynasty love poems to the electric passion of Walt Whitman, from Plato to *Orlando* – queer identity has been at the vibrant centre of our experience. We believe that a profound engagement with queer history is vital to the future of our community. Without roots, progress is always in danger of being lost.

Queer Was Always Here is thrilled to be partnering with The Lot in its production of *What It Means*, which with enormous eloquence and compassion explores that intersection between history and the future. Merle Miller's remarkable life and work remain fiercely urgent.

To learn more about who we are, or to donate, visit our website by scanning below or find us on Instagram at @queerwasalwayshere!

WILTON'S

MUSIC HALL

About Wilton's Music Hall

Wilton's is of international significance as it is the only surviving grand music hall in the world.

Wilton's has been a Grade II listed building since 1971 and is situated in a conservation area.

Wilton's was built in 1858 by the entrepreneur John Wilton. In the 1880s fire regulations changed and it closed as a music hall. It was purchased by a Wesleyan Mission and used by them until the 1950s.

The Methodists departed in 1950 and the building fell into disrepair despite a failed restoration attempt in the 1980s, which actually left the building gutted and structurally dangerous.

In 2023 the picture has changed somewhat. In 2015 we completed a three-year Heritage Lottery Funded capital project, which has conserved the hall, maintaining the beautiful barley twist columns and the handsome balcony. After the completion of work on the hall the houses were then restored ensuring that Wilton's had more front of house and commercial space as well as dedicated learning facilities.

Wilton's is now home to a year-round programme of extraordinary theatre and music, made for all of London and everyone with a curious imagination. Our building is now open and accessible every weekday, with an affordable artistic programme running all year round, which has included work by English National Opera, Kneehigh, BalletBoyz and Watermill Theatre to name but a few.

For more information about Wilton's Music Hall visit

www.wiltons.org.uk

What It Means

For my husband.

Characters

Merle Miller, *writer, an Iowan who escaped.*
Boy from Pittsburgh, *seventeen years old.*

All other voices are played by **Merle**.

Setting

The Glass House, Brewster, New York.

The action takes place from June 1970 to June 1971. Everything else is memory.

Notes on the text

For the purpose of drama, I've broadened out some of the periphery characters. I'm sure Merle – who loved and appreciated the theatre – will understand.

/ denotes an overlap in the text.

1. That Isn't Me

Sunday 28 June 1970.

In New York City, the world's first Gay Pride is taking place.

Fifty miles north east, nestled in the pines, sits a glass house, reflecting the brilliant midday sunshine. We are in Merle's studio: books, a desk, a typewriter and an old TV set. Perched on the shelf, overlooking the action, a fish tank – many tropical fish inside.

Chanting of 'Gay is good, Gay is proud' and other voices blow in from outside – distant, but heard.

A door flings open, Tchaikovsky's Piano Concerto No. 1 in B-Flat Minor booms into the room and **Merle Miller** *– bespectacled, beleaguered – stands in his dressing gown and jiffy slippers; he is holding a coffee pot and has* The New York Times *tucked under his arm.*

He shuffles in.

Merle (*to the typewriter*)   I'm here, don't panic, I'm here. God awful night. (*Throwing the paper on the desk.*) God awful world, it turns out . . . (*Looking over yesterday's work.*) You see, it's not so bad . . .

He picks up the wastepaper basket beneath the desk. He goes around the room, fishing out the cigarette butts from all the ash trays and clearing empty bottles.

I need order right now, please. Cleanliness and . . .

Gentleness.

Quite a harsh light. It would do better if it were cloudy. Greyer. Less brilliant.

And we need the rain . . .

A noise from downstairs.

Huh?

He removes the bin from the room. He then takes off his glasses, wipes them and puts them on again.

Beat.

Something's off.

He notices the fish tank.

Oh for God's . . . (*Going to the fish tank.*) . . . third one this month . . . (*Fishing out the dead fish.*) You can't all be that *sensitive* . . . you get the best food, the best . . . Don't think you're getting a burial.

You'll be a delicious hors d'oeuvre for the birds.

He opens the sliding door to the outside world. He takes a few steps out and flings the fish away.

Be free.

A moment. He hears the protest from afar.

That was today, wasn't it. What's the day again? They all fuse together in the hot months . . .

Gay Liberation Day. That's it. Gay Liberation Day . . .

He takes in the audience.

Oh yes, you're here. That's happening.

He straightens up, perhaps more self-conscious than before.

Well, fine . . . after you.

He holds the space for the audience, and then goes back into the house.

'There it was, out at last. And if it seems like nothing very much, I can only say that it took me a long time to say it, to be able to say it, and none of the journey was easy.'

. . .

Not my words.

Words of the protagonist. George. George Lionel. From my book.

(*Correcting himself.*) From my novel.

I'm writing a novel – my eleventh. Three years in and maybe, nearly, done.

He's a special one. George. Well, all my characters are special, but he is, for the first time, a very special one. One of them. One of the (*looking out to the beyond*) one of *those*.

As am I. I guess we better get that out the way first. That's why you're here. To observe, to learn, to understand . . .

He puts some paper in the typewriter.

My typewriter: efficient, consistent; has issues with the letter k.

(*Flicking through his manuscript.*) I won't reveal the plot – of my novel . . . That is to say it's about someone brilliant who can't handle themselves and the world around them and so decides to end it.

Himself. (*Makes a gun sound.*)

Probably a bit too devasting, I'm sure, but . . . (*Getting distracted by the newspaper.*)

. . . it's what comes out . . .

He picks up the newspaper.

We have another one!

Kate Millett, author of *Sexual Politics*, comes out to the Daughters of Bilitis – the first lesbian organisation. (*Reads.*) 'I'm very glad to be here. It's been kind of a long trip . . . I've wanted to be here, I suppose in a surreptitious way for a long time, and I was always too chicken . . . Anyway, I'm out of the closet. Here I am.'

There you are . . .

Beat.

It's one thing to confess to political unorthodoxy, but to admit sexual unorthodoxy . . . (*Putting the paper down.*)

No.

No, I personally have no taste for 'self-revelation'.

It's all a bit – airing one's private life.

'Surreptitious' . . .

Well, she can't rely on book sales.

No. I prefer to keep it within these four walls. Let it flavour my work, let it be the seasoning, the something unsaid, the unknowable.

Emily Dickinson. 'Tell all the truth but tell it slant.'

I digress.

He sits to write. The march enters the room again, 'We Shall Overcome'.

Must be quite a crowd.

Small at first. The brave ones out front, with their banners. Heads up, chests high. Painted faces. And the others, on the fringes, who slowly, one by one, join the great train.

In the end, between five and fifteen thousand people marched up Sixth Avenue, from Sheridan Square to the Sheep Meadow in Central Park. To the most almighty 'gay-in'.

Other, smaller, parades took place in Chicago and Los Angeles.

And all three cities survived the sight and sound of men with their arms around men and women kissing women, chanting – well, we can all hear the chanting – (*standing and shouting*) I hear you, alright, I hear you!

He shuts the sliding door.

'We shall overcome.'

Jesus.

The chanting stops.

A year ago today

I had a friend who was there that night. At the Stonewall Inn. He said it was beautiful. The sissies fought back! They pulled up parking meters, threw rocks and coins at the cops – the whole thing spearheaded by those who had the least. Isn't that the way. Marsha P. Johnson, Sylvia Rivera – someone give them a medal . . .

I was here, probably. Definitely. Sweating out the novel.

It was a hot night, I remember that. It's always hot when there's a riot.

Riot? We're in the middle of a freaking fag revolution – say the politicians – one that will prove fatal to American society, if not the world.

They love to trash us. It gets the scared vote. We're a country of terrified people.

How sad.

I must say, you're a terrific distraction.

He sits.

Beat.

Did I eat? I am hungry. David? (*He stamps his foot.*) David – a writer, too, younger than me – not too much younger – he prefers it down there. In his lair. We're less on each other's tails.

At my age, one demands space.

And that's just it: gay radicalism is for the young – which isn't to say I haven't been a radical. In fact, I am – more closely akin to the new left than the old.

Listen.

I'm a member of twenty-two organisations *devoted* to improving the lot of the world's outcasts.

I'm the first one to sign a petition for this good cause or that.

And I had no problem in returning my two bronze stars for bravery in combat. Which is exactly what I did. In protest at the Vietnam War.

Two – with clusters.

And, sure, I'm not adverse to marching.

But I am to crusades.

I'm done with crusades.

They're tiring, they age you and right now my principal concerns are more for my digestion than for politics – or sex.

I'm not even sure it's a proper subject for such a thing . . . who was it who said . . .

'I hate the idea of causes. And if I had to choose between betraying my country and betraying my friend, I hope I would have the guts to betray my country.'

E.M. Forster.

From his essay 'What I Believe'.

Now he was a gutsy man.

It took courage to write those words, just as it does, at times, for anyone else to repeat them.

Once I wanted to use them on the title page of a book I wrote. I was advised against it. Why ask for more trouble, they said, I was trouble enough – a liberal screenwriter – plus I was on the list – Senator McCarthy's list that is. So I better roll with the tide – that was the saying then – roll with the tide!

I'm still waiting for that damn tide to subside . . .

E.M. Forster was not a man who rolled with the tide. I met him twice, heard him lecture several times, was acquainted with several of his friends, and knew that he was a . . .

He breaks away, distracted.

I'm jumping around. If you want to stay and watch, fine. I live in a glass house, my glass mausoleum as its affectionately been called, and I have no problem being seen. What queen do you know who doesn't love to be seen?

We take an audience with us wherever we go. We're not picky. And you're not special.

It's just how it is.

At least when you're close, we can hear what you're saying about us.

(*Inspired.*) A fag is a homosexual who has just left the room.

He laughs.

Not that I give anyone the chance. Out here. In the woods. Hidden. I'm a good fifteen minutes from the village. And a good fifty miles from . . . all that.

Here there a few held breaths at the village grocery store. But out there, in the city? There are all the eyes, all the tuts, all the people. The sound of handcuffs is never far away.

I know it shouldn't bother me. That's what everybody says, 'Don't let it bother you'.

But it does.

It bothers me every time I enter a room. Friend or foe? Is there a difference?

(*Pointing to the protesters beyond.*) They don't give a damn whether people like them or not. They just want the rights they're entitled to.

Well, I'm afraid I want both. I dislike being despised.

He pours himself a coffee.

Second pot.

That's not to say I'm not rooting. Of course, I'm rooting, but
. . . activism has changed, it's accelerated, everything has
accelerated, and I don't know the rules anymore. I'm not
even sure I'm allowed to play.

(*Pretending, trying.*) We shall overcome!

A moment.

And this?

Each novel a minimum of three years. A commissioned
article? Meticulous research. Months of wrangling, of
working in isolation. The result?

I'm that safe pair hands, trustworthy –

And a war hero to boot . . .

Two bronze stars.

Look at me, giving my own eulogy . . . it's because you're
here, I can't help it.

He looks out to the beyond.

Still, it might be nice to go. See what the young are wearing.
David can drive us to the station – I am one of the non-
driving minority – then the train to Manhattan, hour
thirty-two . . . Two o'clock, three o'clock, four o'clock . . . be
back in time for dinner. I'm defrosting that duck . . . it would
all work.

*He has a pain in his stomach, a familiar pain. He breathes
into it.*

No.

It's too late now for radical shifts of character. I am afraid I
will have to make do with me.

Which is what Mother said in the beginning.

My place is here. This is where I'm useful.

The truth is I have never felt comfortable in those places, those bars . . . Listen to me having to defend myself!

I have nothing to defend.

Gay radicalism is for the young, and I have a story to write.

He sits down and types. The chanting breaks in again and a shadow passes the house.

2. The Article

September 1970.

Evening.

In the news: Harper's Magazine *publishes a ten thousand-word polemic by academic Joseph Epstein called 'Homo/Hetero: The Struggle for Sexual Identity'. The front cover shows a white man's muscular chest stretching through a woman's red blouse.*

Merle *is typing.*

Merle (*to the audience*)   Most serious writers write slowly.

And thus miss deadlines.

Sometimes several deadlines – publishers' deadlines that is.

A serious writer cannot have any serious deadline but their own.

The phone rings.

And they cannot have these goddamn interruptions –

I'm not in!

He's never in.

Don't they know that by now . . .

The phone keeps ringing.

Goddamn it, answer the phone, David . . .!

He breaks away from his desk.

(*To the audience.*) It is my experience that whenever the word 'homosexual' is printed in a newspaper or magazine, the phone positively flies off its handle.

Especially when it's *Harper's Magazine* – one of the best, maybe the best, magazine in the country – I used to be its editor – and they – the gossips, the insecure vampires – they can smell my spiked adrenaline, and they all want to feed.

I answer.

They say what do you think?

I say it's six pages too long.

The article in question, 'Homo/Hetero: The Struggle for Sexual Identity', an eleven-page polemic by 'proclaimed liberal' and passionate heterosexual Joseph Epstein. Thirty-three. Like I said, eleven pages.

I say who's the beefcake on the front?

They draw me back to the content.

I quote the content, 'They are different from the rest of us . . . cursed without clear cause, afflicted without apparent cure, they are an affront to our rationality' . . .

They say powerful, huh?

I say without doubt the most blatant, bigoted piece – full of the most juvenile mistakes – I have ever read.

They say they found it illuminating.

I quote, 'I must have been nine or ten years old when my father sat me down to explain there were perverts in the world. These were men with strange appetites, men whose minds were twisted –'

They say no not that bit.

I quote, 'If I had the power to do so, I would wish homosexuality off the face of this earth. I would do so because I think that it brings infinitely more pain than pleasure to those who are forced to live with it.'

They go quiet.

I say this writer is advocating genocide for homosexuals.

They say don't be ridiculous

I quote, 'I would wish homosexuality off the face of this earth.'

They say let me read it again –

I say, what do you not understand?

They say, side issue, what's really important right now is the feminist movement.

I say what about the rights of the lesbians within the feminist movement?

They say, you should know I'm not a lesbian.

I say it wouldn't matter if you were.

They cut off.

Hello?

And now I ring them. The straights. Searching for one to feel the way I do. For someone to recognise the cruelty.

We all recognise cruelty, don't we?

They say you have to allow difference of opinion.

I hang the fuck up.

And I've digressed.

'Confusion, revulsion, fear . . .'

He goes to the phone. He dials a number.

Finally I ring my old boss and friend of twenty-five years Bob Kotlowitz, executive editor of *Harper's*. I've always seen him as a brave and generous man. He'll understand.

> **Merle** (*on the phone*)   Bob, the Epstein article is an outrage.

Merle, *not for the first time, becomes someone else.*

> **Bob**   A great many intelligent people feel the way that he does, Merle.

> **Merle**   Do you feel that way?

A moment.

Bob   Oh, I suppose, more or less.

That was the time for me to have said, 'After all these years, is that what you think of me?' But I didn't. The moment passed. It passed as it had passed so many hundred times before.

But this anger hadn't.

It was staying with me, here – hot.

Merle *sits down and serves coffee and cheesecake.*

    Elinor   I think it's tedious.

My ex-wife, Elinor. She came over for coffee and cheesecake and we read the article together. It was Labour Day weekend. For some reason that detail is important. Maybe it was the sound of the local brass band blowing in – Americana never sounded so conceited.

    Merle   It's more than that, it's –

    Elinor   Outrageous, harmful and hurtful. All those things. But what can one do?

I realised then that in all the years I've known her – almost twenty-five, married for more than four – we had never discussed the subject of homosexuality. Never mentioned my own

    Merle   Elinor, did I ever tell you –

    Elinor   It's the crumb, the crumb is excellent, truly.

    Merle   It's graham crackers.

    Elinor   Is that right? Huh.

The moment passed again.

I read somewhere when you keep one part of yourself secret for so long, it becomes the most important part of you. That, I believe, is an absolute truth.

In fact, it may be the most important truth of all.

3. French Restaurant

Merle   A week goes by and I'm sitting in a French restaurant having lunch with a couple of big wigs from *The New York Times Magazine*. Let's call them Victor and Gerry – fast talkers, slow eaters.

> **Merle**   It was just page after page of horror. Listen – 'I cannot get over the brutally simple fact that two men make love to each other.'
>
> **Victor**   It's selling *a lot* of copies. They're on the third rollout already.
>
> **Merle**   But what did you think of the article, Victor?
>
> **Victor**   I thought it was brilliant.
>
> **Merle**   . . .
>
> **Victor**   At a time when everybody is saying we have to understand and accept homosexuals, Epstein is saying –
>
> **Merle** (*standing up*)   Epstein is saying genocide for queers.
>
> *The hum of the restaurant stops, the world goes quiet.*

And this was the moment. I'm near half way through my life. I have terrible eyesight, relentless ambition and, in broad daylight, before what I guess you call a mixed audience, in a French restaurant on West 46th Street, I found myself saying –

> **Merle**   Look, goddamn it, I'm a homosexual, the man I live with is a homosexual and some of my best friends are homosexuals, and I am sick and tired of reading and hearing such goddamn degrading bullshit about me and my friends.

There it was, out at last, and if it seemed like nothing very much, I can only say that it took me a long time to say it, to

be able to say it, and none of the journey was easy . . .
(*realising*) Oh . . . they were my words.

Back in the restaurant. I sit down, readjust my napkin and
take a sizeable gulp of my Cabernet Franc. My friends' jaws
are on the floor, but I'm focusing on finishing my coq au vin
and pocketing all the luxury soaps from the bathroom – who
knows when I'll be back here again.

4. Masks

The Glass House.

Evening. Rain.

Merle *goes and pours himself a large whisky.*

Merle   Finally, rain.

I think Tchaikovsky for now.

Nothing too bombastic.

Something laboured and pained.

Full of regret.

To go with –

The dispiriting months.

One of the sadder symphonies comes on.

Good.

Fiftysomething years, and finally the fag leaves the room.

To an unnamed wood.

Here.

Home.

Cheers.

He drinks.

Had I said too much?

Or not enough?

What a fink I was!

To take all this time . . .

Why was I always bothered?

He starts to undress.

It's important to establish now that I'm not adverse to fun.

And with David out the house . . .

I don't know where he goes.

I've had plenty of parties for one.

He goes to his closet. He changes into his Halloween outfit – a Bigfoot all-in-one costume; it's freaky.

I'm not crazy about Bigfoot, but I relate to her outsider status. And her need for solitude.

And it's cosy.

She's out there.

I believe.

A moment.

When I was a child in Marshalltown, Iowa, I hated Christmas, but I loved Halloween. I never wanted to take off the mask. I wanted to wear it everywhere, night and day, always . . .

Merle, *as Bigfoot, gets a bowl of candy by the shelf. He opens the glass door, waiting for the trick or treaters.*

And I suppose I still do.

(*Shaking the candy.*) Trick or treat?

Here they come . . .

    Victor Merle!

Merle It's Victor from 'the lunch'. He's accosting me by a photocopier –

    Victor I've been thinking about some of the things you said at the lunch. Brilliant. You knocked the wind right out of us – we couldn't stop talking about it in the office.

Merle Oh, well, at least I was brilliant.

Victor   And, Merle, we have a proposition for you.
Would you be willing to write a piece on it?

Merle   A piece on –

Victor   You know, you being a –

Merle   The words ricochet around *The New York Times*
offices –

Victor   – A fruit, a flit, a floozy – call it what you want,
you're the writer. What do you say?

Merle   I mumble something of a –

Victor   It's a response piece. But more than that, it's
. . . we want this to be about the changing attitudes
towards homosexuality, your own included – make it as
personal as you like.

Merle   Personal, really.

Victor   Defend being who you are. But don't
proselytise. I don't want you lining up recruits. Now as
the very nature of the article is hazardous, we may not
run with it. But try it anyhow. You'll get a kill fee. You
have three weeks, Merle. Three. Make it a good one.

Merle *closes the sliding the door.*

Merle   My habit of saying yes and then immediately
regretting it is something I'm working on.

Make it as personal as you like?

Code for self-pitying as possible.

He takes off the mask. He's gone hot.

I tend to run a little anxious, but this . . .

He sits and eats the candy.

'Your own experience included' . . .

Once you've scraped away all the lies and embellishments
. . .

We're just left with ourselves.

And I'd rather not make do with that.

He goes to the drinks cabinet and pours himself another.

Why not? It's my coming-out party after all.

I don't drink for inspiration. I have enough of that.

I drink for when the vampires descend.

And they do.

They say they won't be able to see me again if I write
something like this.

I say but it's the *Times*.

They say especially if it's in the *Times*!

I say I think it's important to do it.

They say we all get angry at injustice –

(*Passionate.*) I say damn right – we should be angry –
constantly – always!

They say, but is the *Times* the right place for this anger?

I say it's exactly the right place – and you're just jealous!

They say, well, I hope you're prepared for the consequences.

I say I will need friends at this time.

They say we're not friends anymore.

I say, well, good!

He throws his glass against the wall. It doesn't smash.

Plastic. We've learnt our lesson.

Why would I *do* such a thing? The great sissy from Iowa!
Would people even care?

He searches his desk for the Valium.

Before starting an opinion piece, a calm mind is imperative for a healthy argument.

(*Shaking the bottle of Valium.*) Just a couple.

They help take the edge off.

He takes a couple of downers.

Everything is ok.

Personal? I can excavate.

For sure, it's been a wonderful life . . .

> **Merle**   Hello, Mother, I've been commissioned.
>
> **Mother**   Doesn't matter if they don't run with it.
>
> **Merle**   It's for the *Times*.
>
> **Mother**   Why you want to write for these liberal washy papers, I don't know.
>
> **Merle**   They think I'm brilliant.
>
> **Mother**   Brilliant people don't hide in the woods, writing stories. Especially personal ones.
>
> **Merle**   But you always told me to tell the truth.
>
> **Mother**   The truth is, prejudice is in-built. A natural part of the human psyche. And more fool you for subjecting yourself to it.
>
> **Merle**   . . .
>
> **Mother**   And, afterwards, don't come home, your tail between your legs, crying to me.

The sound of freight train far off – distant, haunting.

What an elaborate charade.

It's as one of my favourite queens said, 'Straights don't want to know, and they can never forgive you for telling them. They prefer to think it doesn't exist.'

I'm here to tell you it does. In *The New York Times*.

'I would never consider a person healthy unless they had overcome prejudice against homosexuality.'

Who said that?

Beat.

George. Another George perhaps.

Why are they all called George?

It's not too late, is it?

Well, I guess I should start with figuring out what *causes* it.

I have spent several thousand dollars and several thousand hours with various therapists. And while they have often been helpful in leading me to an understanding of how I got to be the way I am, none of them had any feasible, to me feasible, suggestion as to how I could be any different.

And they all agree *it* is a mental illness. So there's that.

Beat.

When the fear creeps in again, I turn to pot.

He rolls a spliff.

I had one – white jeans, pearls, expensive shoes – who claimed not only that she could 'cure' me but also rid me of my writer's block. She did neither.

I'm afraid I'll have to make do with me.

He lights his spliff.

Isn't that right . . .

Mother?

A freight train careers through the rural Iowa countryside. It sounds its horn and **Merle** *gets high.*

5. The Horror

October 1970.

In New York City, members of the Gay Activists Alliance stage an all-day sit-in at the Harper's *offices to protest against the Epstein article.*

Merle *is passed out on the couch.*

The phone rings.

Merle (*sudden*)   I'm up.

David?

The phone?

Hello?

But the train has left the station.

I answer

They say where are you?

I say who is this?

They say The GAA

The Gay Activists Alliance are ringing me. How did they –

They say they've broken into the offices of *Harper's Magazine* – dear Lord – and are a staging a sit-in.

I say a what?

They say – they *shout* – A SIT-IN – to protest the Epstein article. And why the hell aren't I there?

I say, I say, I'm writing an article – on all of it – lead piece.

They say no article – no – they need my presence – to talk to Bob – the editor – to be a buffer

I say I can't do anything – I'm not – I need to wait for David – live very far – ah – won't make a difference – but maybe my written response? – my personal response? . . .

And they've gone.

They've gone.

Of course. They're militant, they're brilliant, they're new.

They've broken in?

Ok. Fine.

They sit there, I sit here.

He sits at his typewriter, putting the paper in.

There are many ways to protest.

I'm searching for the truth here!

I am writing an article

on what it means to be a . . .

Start with an apology.

(Typing.) Apologies in advance but I will largely be speaking about male homosexuality, which has been my experience.

Ok. No one can attack me now.

The phone rings again.

He's not *in*!

They say – they shout – Merle! Was this your goddamn idea?

I say, no, Bob-editor-of-Harper's-Magazine, it most certainly was not.

Bob says there's got to be a hundred of them – won't get off the damn floor – offering coffee and doughnuts and God knows what else.

I say try listening to them – read a pamphlet!

Bob says where did you catch it?

I say you can't catch it, it's innate.

Bob says something cruel.

I say a number.

And Bob hangs up.

But I remember the number – thirty-seven per cent.

He scans his bookshelf.

K, K, Kinsey, Dr C . . . recent desecrator of America's sexual puritanism and emphatic data queen . . .

Dr Alfred C. Kinsey said that thirty-seven per cent of all males have had or at least will have one homosexual experience between adolescence and old age.

Hear the silence in the room!

Thirty-seven per cent. A number recently confirmed again in a nationwide poll. Well, a *Psychology Today* poll.

Up the smarts a bit, Merle, it's the *Times*.

Voltaire is said to have had one such experience, with an Englishman. When the Englishman suggested they do it again, Voltaire replied,

> **Voltaire**   If you try it once, you're a philosopher; if twice, you are a sodomite.

I've always hated Voltaire.

People prefer practicalities. We're a practical country. The US Census. The US Census!

We were ignored in the census – lesbian, bi, transgender – not one bit of official data . . . we're miasma . . . avoided . . . spectres . . . we cling onto the few surveys like buoys in the vast ocean –

Merle *opens the drawers, searching for data.*

Three to four million Americans – National Institute of Mental Health – could be, maybe, are . . .

One in four, one in six – tendencies

Sixty-three per cent hate us! We're 'harmful' to American society . . .

And somehow, I'm up to the task of persuading them otherwise?

He pulls out a lavender sachet. He breathes into it deeply.

Lavender. It's calming. For my system.

Here, (*throwing the sachet to an audience member*) a gift. Something to remember me by, of when I was in my prime . . .

He undoes the bottom of phone receiver, checking inside for wires.

When vigilance was the name of the game and it didn't matter if you passed . . .

> **McCarthy**   We will rout them out. One by one . . .

Senator McCarthy – remember him? – was not a fan of lavender. He loved attacking us as much as communists – claiming we were often the same. A special police squad was set up –

> **McCarthy**   To investigate the links between homosexuality and communism. We will rout them out, one by one.

Hundreds of people accused of homosexual acts were fired from all kinds of government posts.

And they watched and did nothing.

The American Civil Liberties Union. Notably silent. And most silent of all was a closet queen who was a member of the board of directors.

Myself.

Change the system from within – how naive –

Solidarity equalled annihilation, you're either in or you're out, there was no . . .

No excuse.

At a time for flourish and flair how many of us were held up by the red light?

Our courage was bent to stoicism.

Beat.

(*Meaning it.*) If you could only understand the fear.

Merle *slams the receiver down.*

>   **McCarthy**   We will rout them out. One by one . . .

Merle *spots someone through the window.*

Oh, the inquisitive postman again. (*Calling out.*) Had a good read of them, have you? Give them a better lick next time, yes?

He surveys the room for other threats.

The phone rings, he jumps.

They want you nervous, they want you jumpy . . .

(*Relief.*) An old friend.

They say about this weekend –

I say I'm looking forward to seeing them.

They say they've changed their mind about bringing John.

That's their sixteen-year-old son.

I say, oh no, is he sick?

They say – they've read the Epstein piece –

I say, ok . . .

They say, the thing is, Merle –

I see where this is going.

He's an impressionable kid, and while they know I wouldn't –

I try to . . . formulate –

They say what if I had some friends in and they try to make a pass at him?

I firmly suggest they not come for the weekend.

The great fear.

To think it's contagious, floating in the air, like a virus.

> **Martin Hoffman**   We assume that heterosexual arousal is somehow natural and needs no explanation.

Martin Hoffman, a voice of reason within the madness.

And I quote, 'To call it natural evades the whole issue; it is as if we said it's natural for the sun to come up in the morning and left it at that. Is it possible we know less about human sexuality than the medieval astrologers knew about the stars?'

Mother   The truth is, prejudice is in-built.

Merle   Go away, Mother.

Mother   A natural part of the human psyche.

Wine or a pill?

Merle *takes both*.

Stonewall was only a year ago. Should I chart their progress from then till now? Keep it sociological; less personal –

The phone rings.

(*Furious.*) Oh my GOD, I can't DO this.

But it's the GAA again –

I say how's it going?

They say Bob is threatening to call the cops.

I say relax. Bob won't call the cops. He won't want the headlines. You stay where you are.

And they've gone.

But I've chosen my team . . .

He reaches for the dictionary.

A, a, ally . . . (*reading*) a person or organisation that cooperates . . .

I know what it means!

So why do I feel so alone?

He pulls out the paper from the typewriter.

None of this will serve anyone.

He screws the paper up, throws it into the fireplace.

And silence is a habit.

Dinner.

He pulls his desk centre and gets out two place mats, two candles, two glasses and two plates. He neatly arranges them. He pours himself another drink.

He puts on a pair of oven mitts and gets out a hotpot. He places it on the table.

Hotpot. Not my finest, but it's a Tuesday.

He waits.

He's late.

*From afar, we hear the sound of **Young Merle** practising the piano.*

(*Stirring the hotpot.*) It's getting cold. Goddammit, David . . .

He paces the room.

Nothing I've written has come easily.

I believe Ben Jonson when he says that Shakespeare never blotted a line. I believe that Mozart composed the overture to Don Giovanni while the first-night audience were walking into the theatre.

And I believe this should be easier.

I'm practising the piano between ten and twelve hours a day. Back tense, shoulders high, Mother hearing every mistake. I can see I will never be another Wolfgang Amadeus. I'm now sixteen and I've decided it was either that – brilliance – prodigy – genius – or nothing.

Young Merle *slams down the piano lid.*

Nothing!

Mozart plays – something stressed from Figaro. *A car swings into the driveway.*

Merle (*an explosion of rage*)   Oh for God's sake. Now he arrives? No. That is it. That is it! He's late. He's late! He can't have it. You can't have it!

He opens the sliding door.

(*Yelling.*) When I say eight, I mean eight! If you want someone patient –

He grabs the hotpot and throws it in the bin, followed by the plates, candlesticks and all.

I'm not that guy.

To hell with you!

You ruined it!

It was perfect.

He goes to the door to the living area.

And I will not be disturbed.

He goes with a slam.

Over in the fireplace, the paper ignites. A huge fire burns bright, and all the books fall from the shelves.

6. Aristocracy of the Sensitive

The next morning.

Outside it's close to freezing. Inside, the fire is still burning.

Merle *shuffles in carrying the self-inflicted wounds from last night. He goes to feed the fish.*

Merle   Still alive. (*Taking in the messy room.*) I stopped a novel for this? It's all part of the creative process, all part. (*Picking up the books.*) Perfectly normal. Some nuts are harder to crack. The trick is not to be too rigid, but let your mind be open for the . . . (*taking in the audience*) for the . . .

He pulls out a notice from the shelf that reads: 'GO HOME. I AM NOT WORKING TODAY.' He stands, quietly holding it.

I didn't talk much last night. I let him do the talking.

The clear-up.

That's what he does. So well.

I slept – deeply, in fact, it was . . .

What was it he said?

It was about someone. Someone a very long time ago who went through something very similar.

David read about it in the *Times* – how's that for irony – they can't get enough of us.

E.M. Forster's posthumous novel *Maurice*, completed in 1915, will, after fifty-five years, be published. E.M. Forster kept the novel hidden from the world.

On top of his manuscript he wrote: 'Publishable – but is it worth it?'

> **E.M. Forster**   I believe in aristocracy . . . not an aristocracy of power, based upon rank and influence, but an aristocracy of the sensitive, the considerate, and the plucky. Its members are to be found in all nations

and classes, and through all ages, and there is a secret understanding between them when they meet. They represent the human tradition, the one queer victory of our race over cruelty and chaos.

Is it worth it?

Even so courageous a man as Forster had to ask himself that question.

A moment.

And yet cruelty and chaos are all that I bring, all I seem capable of –

Stop.

The train has left the station.

It left a long time ago.

What's my excuse?

Merle *goes to the typewriter and starts typing. The freight train again, and rural Iowa fills the room.*

7. The Birth of Sissy

Merle, *walking through memory.*

All my mother ever wanted was

> **Mother**   A little girl, to dress up in pink, to give a little colour to the proceedings.

And she sighed.

She was a sigher.

> **Mother**   But we love you just the same.

Only I didn't believe it.

Not for a minute.

> **Elinor**   I cannot understand why you would say something like that –
>
> **Merle**   You might wait till I'm back from Europe to explain myself –
>
> **Elinor**   You make it impossible for me not to feel inadequate –
>
> **Merle**   Elinor, don't talk like this –
>
> **Elinor**   But for you to spread lies, lies which I have to clear up –
>
> **Merle**   You don't – I'll sort it –
>
> **Elinor**   Are you ashamed of me?

Merle   Hurt.

Betrayed.

> **Elinor**   Why?

Every question mark, a scream –

> **Merle**   This writing is illegible, Elinor.

He puts away the letter in his pocket.

She's not pregnant.

My wife.

A Friend   Two years, no baby?

People were asking questions –

Merle   Well, actually –

A lie.

A lie to get through the day.

To pass.

To be convincing.

And she found out.

I'm slipping –

Little Old Lady   What an adorable little girl!

Pink. My baby blankets were all pink, purchased before the disaster, my birth. The lace on my baby dress was pink; my bonnet was fringed with pink – and my hair was long and lusterless.

Little Old Lady   How old is she?

And they find out that *he* was born screaming in May 1917; and that he's been screaming ever since.

I learnt to dignify the scream.

Quieten it.

Keep it inside.

I've been bloated all this time.

Mother (*sighing*)   It's a boy.

Not the plan.

Mother   We're disappointed. But we'll have to make do.

Our family motto. Make do. It wasn't enough to live in a run-down rooming house on the wrong side of Marshalltown, Iowa – we had to also make do with the Great Depression and its limited horizons –

And me.

All my mother ever wanted was

> **Mother**   A little girl, to dress up in pink, to give a little colour to the proceedings.

> **Little Old Lady**   How old is she?

They kept on saying that until I got my first butch haircut at four years old.

Not until college did I read that Oscar Wilde's mother started him down the garden path by letting his hair grow and dressing him as a little girl. As Oscar said,

> **Oscar Wilde**   Children begin by loving their parents; as they grow older, they judge them; sometimes they forgive them.

My father –

> **Mother**   A total failure.

And she was right on that, lost all our money in the Florida land boom, and once we got poor, we stayed poor.

> **Mother**   You'll have wing for supper, and tomorrow you can take the leg –

A chicken rationed to its every inch. Day-old bread, holes in all my shoes, hand-me-down clothes from our more prosperous cousins.

Poverty is neither funny nor a breeding a ground for love – at least it wasn't in our house. No colour, no joy, just plenty of blame.

Am I hungry?

Third Grader   Hey, sissy!

I start school a year early –

Mother   He's clever enough –

She wanted me out the house.

Third Grader   Sissy, sissy –

The birth of Sissy. I'm four years old. And it seems to me now that I heard it at least once five days a week for the next thirteen years.

I can't really see where it's coming from.

Mother   You inherited your father's eyes, among other weaknesses.

I'm diagnosed practically blind. I am given steel-rimmed glasses to wear – but they can't possibly be right because all I seem to be seeing is scowls . . .

It's then I start to see what is so upsetting to other people.

Elinor   I cannot understand why you would say something like that.

It was better when I was blind.

Army Psychiatrist   I'm going to ask you a few questions and then I'm going to hit your knee with this little hammer, alright?

The draft had come in and I was first in line.

Army Psychiatrist   How do you feel about girls, Mr Miller?

Merle *looks up the army psychiatrist's eyes, resolute.*

And I'm sworn into the army.

Well.

Not the army

I'm a reporter for *Yank* magazine – the army's weekly publication.

But it was my way in.

Doing what I'm good at in the costume of a soldier.

Look at me.

I'm on a boat, in the Pacific. We're approaching the island, I'm surrounded by men, and bullets. We're in fog, deep fog, we're landing. This is happening. I feel the heat of the mortar fire, I see it hit human flesh, and I smell, oh the smell, I'm running, Both sides are fighting for something they can't grasp and,

I'm writing everything down.

And I'm called brave.

I'm dodging bullets.

My feet go to the right place at the right time.

How are they missing me?

I seemed to have nine lives, taking them all from the men around me, the young and bewildered men.

All the wrong people die, I do believe that.

The enemy stops firing. **Merle** *takes off his helmet.*

Who was I doing this for?

The great sissy from Iowa.

I'm standing in a field. It's baseball time at school. I skirt around the edge of the pitch, willing time to speed up when the unthinkable happens.

The ball is hit high in the air.

It's coming right at me.

I have to catch the thing. This is what men do. They catch balls.

Why

Is this happening?

My team take a collective in-breath

The ball is getting closer but in that moment I see the clouds beyond it . . . drifting, oblivious and free . . . doing their own thing . . . despite my turmoil . . . and I think . . . how delightful it would be . . . to glide through life . . . to not . . . be . . .

> *The pitch groans.*

> **Third Grader**   Pansy.

> **Fourth Grader**   Fairy.

> **Fifth Grader**   Nance.

> **Sixth Grader**   Fruit.

> **Seventh Grader**   Fruitcake.

I hear you all.

> **Adult**   Faggot.

No – faggot is later.

A doorbell sounds.

When I wasn't in class, they – the bullies – would get creative. One Easter weekend there, addressed to me, was a beautiful-looking basket; inside a bunch of faeces. Does one say a bunch of faeces? What is the collective noun for faeces . . .?

It was one hell of an Easter surprise.

A mother's scream is heard far-off.

Children spot difference before anyone.

I quit piano.

I quit violin.

> **Third Grader**   Sissy –

Once a day, five days a week, thirteen years.

Undersized, under-nourished, I decided to eat nothing but Wheaties – hoping to turn into another Jack Armstrong.

I bought all the body-building equipment Charles Atlas had to offer, but it did no good. I remained an eighty-nine-pound weakling year after year . . .

Boy   You're going to be a fag when you grow up.

They also looked right at me when they said the words. Funny, that which was inconceivable to me was for them common sense, a matter of fact – fixed.

The only thing I can think to my credit is that I almost never ran away.

I almost always stared them down.

I cried later. When I was alone.

Five days a week

Thirteen years

He rearranges his posture.

And then I finally got it – be someone else.

Radio Announcer   So I lowered my voice from uncertain soprano to something two octaves lower and I got a job as a radio announcer. On the airwaves I conjured up an image of smooth, square-jawed all-American male – comforting, familiar. Safe.

Success.

For my next job as city editor of *The Daily Iowan* I played the part of newspaper reporter –

Newspaper Reporter   – a character straight out of *The Front Page*. Wearing a hat indoors and out, talking out of the corner of mouth – never without a cigarette – being folksy with the local cops – whom I detested . . . I chased girls and I denounced queers. Oh yes, I had to be on trend. I trashed them in my columns. I knew

where my kind were likely to hang out – mostly at the
university theatre . . . they wore long hair and I trashed
them for that as well . . . My hair could have grown that
long, if I had let it . . .

(*Meaning it.*) And I would have looked beautiful.

He takes a breath.

It was love I craved, approval, forgiveness for being what I
could not help being. And I have spent a good part of my
adult life looking for those things, always, as a few
psychologists have pointed out, in the places I was least likely
to find them.

> **Elinor**   I cannot understand why you would say
> something like that –

Grey appears. Hair thins.

And then the war is over.

I stay in Europe. Stubbornly sticking to my deepest city-
editor's-radio-announcer's voice as I ordered reporters and
photographers around and kept evenings to myself.

Strict. Split.

What the heck, I've lied this far.

I could see no reason I couldn't be as straight as the next
man.

I served as an editor at *Time* magazine – there were long
conversations – we discovered a British composer was a . . .

I voted against using his picture.

And my second novel had become a bestseller.

(*Not proud.*) My rise within the Establishment was complete.

I was unstoppable. Brilliant, even. And from an angle, with a
squint – yes, I could be a Jack Armstrong. I may not be able
to play baseball, but by God I could and would . . .

I felt it was something I had to do

and I respect her

Love her.

Tchaikovsky's 'Liturgy of St. John Chrysostom: Cherubikon' plays.
Merle *is waiting at the altar;* **Elinor** *joins him – in a red dress.*

Merle *takes out the letter*

> **Elinor**   I cannot understand why you would say
> something like that.

People don't stop questioning.

Tchaikovsky had the same idea. Maybe marriage would cure
him of what he called 'The'. But afterwards, in a letter to a
friend, he wrote –

> **Tchaikovsky**   I saw right away that I could never love
> my wife and that the habit on which I had counted had
> never come. I fell into despair and longed for death . . .
> my mind began to go . . .

Merle *puts on his wedding ring.*

Pytor Ilyich's marriage lasted only two weeks. My own lasted
longer, but my drives were so much stronger than they ever
were before or since that I said I've got to get out of this
situation or it's going to kill me.

It could not have succeeded.

Elinor *dissolves into whiteness.* **Merle** *takes off his ring.*

I'll tell you this. It's not true, that saying about sticks and
stones; it's words that break –

I'm not proud. No, I'm not proud. I'm not proud of my
silence.

I need light.

8. Revolution

Merle *turns on the light. He speaks to the men in the room.*

Merle (*to the audience*)   American men. Men of the world. To all the men in this room – what's your preoccupation with virility?

Lucy Komisar recently got it right in the *Washington Monthly* when she said this country is obsessed with violence and the masculine mystique. The enemies thereof are called 'effete'.

The word means 'sterile, spent, worn-out'.

Effete? That's not in your vocab. It's sissy, fudgepacker, faggot – right?

He lets his wrist go limp.

The limp wrist. How can a relaxed joint strike so much fear in man? What does it conjure up for you?

You're not the first ones to get uptight about such things.

Do I have to?

Fine.

As you're all here.

I'm going to tell you a story. A love story. One of the best.

No, not Romeo and Juliet.

Alexander and Hephaestion.

Now before asking a friend, let me explain . . .

Alexander – Alexander the Great – was bisexual, and he just loved to fuck his best friend, Hephaestion.

And vice versa.

It was joyful time for them. Colonising, sodomising – couldn't be more masculine, you might say.

Only Alexander's daddy got very upset. And blamed the mother of course.

Philip of Macedon   Goddamn it, Olympia, you're making our boy effeminate!

Olympia turned a blind eye, proud of her beautiful boy.

Anyhow, Daddy died and all was well . . . until typhoid came knocking on Hephaestion's door.

The great love was torn asunder, and Alexander went into a tirade of grief.

He immediately crucified the poor physician; ordered all the manes and tails of his horses and mules to be cut; threw down the battlements of the neighboring cities . . . and he banned all flute playing in camp.

Not even the most lavish funeral known to man could soothe his heartbreak.

It was his Achilles heel, as it is for everyone.

When it comes to the heart, are we really so different?

Well, alright, the times were different, are different – attitudes forever shuffling back and forth.

But I would have thought you should have come to a decision by now.

And until then, where can we find a home?

And we're not waiting anymore.

Though some still need to be galvanised.

Thank God for Huey P. Newton, Supreme Commander of the Black Panther Party, who said, 'There is no reason to think a homosexual cannot be revolutionary. Quite the contrary, maybe a homosexual could be the most revolutionary.'

So the answer is revolution. Fine. But in what model?

The newly formed Gay Liberation Front thinks Marxism must be the place. Which is odd because in communist China homosexuals are put in prisons that are called 'hospitals for ideological reform'. And for all those Che Guevara loving folk out there, know this: in Cuba, homosexuals have been placed in concentration camps. Put that on your t-shirt.

Where can we find a home?

I don't know why I'm asking you . . .

Of course, the Soviet Union claims not to have any homosexuals . . .

For a landmass seven times the area of India and two and a half times that of the United States, you have to marvel at the audacity of such claims.

Such stories.

And that people believe them.

But this is what we do, we believe, when someone from up high tells us

Someone powerful

Compelling

A preacher

A politician

A well-known journalist

What's the difference?

And I quote: 'If I had the power to do so, I would wish homosexuality off the face of the earth.'

Tchiakovsky's Swan Lake (*Act Two, Dances des Cygnes*) *creeps in.* **Merle** *goes to the window.*

Is it any wonder when one of the Russian ballet companies come to town . . .

They don't go home?

Nothing pleases me more than hearing Russian voices on West 42nd street.

Courageous voices

Unsilenced

They made the leap.

They sought their freedom.

And they are all, absolutely, welcome here –

Merle *watches the Russian dancers dance. And, with a crescendo, the freight train arrives, and the windows of the glass house steam up.*

9. No Place to Register

Merle, *triumphant, finds himself centre stage: strong, lucid and present.*

Only the music has now stopped. And the glare of the house lights is illuminating all the faces. He feels his posture slipping.

Merle   We can cut the lights now.

The house lights come off. The class of 1934 applaud **Merle***'s speech.*

There I was, at my high school reunion, giving the principal speech to the class of 1934. Yes. I'm back in Marshalltown again. Only this time, I was invited.

Word got out

War hero, best-selling author, acquaintances with Hemingway and Capote . . .

I'm a success.

Success is currency –

    Old Classmate   Oh my God, Merle, look at you now –

– it buys you time.

I make my way down from the podium

I deflect their praise

I undersell, make small talk, laugh – don't want them to feel bad about themselves . . .

And then the band starts up

And everyone finds a dance partner

And suddenly I'm an exposed nerve

With nowhere to hide

But

The band stops playing, a peaceful, warm silence takes over.

The library.

Through my adolescent war, the only place I could escape what I did not understand was the school library.

My mind's thirst for knowledge and understanding is almost as deep as my body's need for another man's touch.

Books.

I had a special set-up with the librarian, a Ms Alice Story – that really was her name – and could take out as many books as I wanted.

I read about sensitive boys, odd boys, boys who were lonely and misunderstood . . . boys who really didn't care that much for baseball, boys who were teased by their classmates . . . books about all of these . . . but in none of them could I find a boy who was tortured by the strange fantasies that tore at me every time I learned how to swim at the 'Y'.

They swam nude at the 'Y'.

Oh why . . .

In gym – required – I always tried to get in and out of the locker room before anybody else arrived . . .

Lead me not into temptation . . .

The band again.

It's my fault for coming back.

When you look back, you get in trouble.

And here's trouble.

A man with a familiar face and an idiot grin is stood in front of me, limp wristed, and saying – loud enough for everyone to hear –

> **Familiar Face** (*in a falsetto*)   How about letting me have this dance, sweetie?

Laughter erupts: the same but middle-aged, crueller;
deepened.

My mouth speaks and I observe it so –

> **Merle**   I'm terribly sorry, but my dance card is
> filled up.

That was the best I could do.

I haul myself to the buffet bar.

I try dancing.

I stand still.

Goddamn it, I've been cut.

They know it, I know it and now they're flocking towards
me. Vulnerability tastes good. And they want to know if
I'm ok.

> **Merle** (*laughing*)   Oh God, it's all nothing but
> gas, right?

My voice sounds higher than usual, I'm sweating, I can't
stop my shoulders from –

Are my eyes watering?

The mask is slipping.

> **Familiar Face** (*in a falsetto*)   How about letting me have
> this dance, sweetie?

They apologise for him.

> **Old Classmate Two**   Rude.

> **Old Classmate Three**   Offensive.

> **Old Classmate Four**   Total bore.

Lip service – how many of them had been tempted to say
the same thing. Or would say something of the kind after
I had gone.

A fag is a homosexual who has left the room.

Even Oscar Wilde. He's been put in the restricted room.

Anyone under forty couldn't get a book out from the restricted room. And so I had to make do with temptation . . .

A train pulls in, passengers leave.

Which was leading me into the Minneapolis & St Louis railroad station . . .

Where I would read odd, frightening things written on the walls of the men's room. Where I would see boys in their teens and early twenties

On their way to and from somewhere on freight cars . . .

Boys who were hungry and jobless

Who needed someone to recognise them

To see them.

Old Classmate Four   Queer.

I'm understanding something but I can't say.

I can never say.

It's easier in the library.

It's safer in the library.

I take out a book called *Thirteen Men*.

I don't recognise the dozen.

But one

One of the men

Kisses his roommate, also male.

A crime, no doubt

Punishable by death.

Now I'm at the railroad.

Because

They never tell you how the body shakes

When it wants something

But it does

It shakes and jumps and flinches

His name was Carl

Carl from Chicago.

His father was a plumber, unemployed

His mother was away, hopefully

Forever

Why don't you go home?

I said

He blew out the smoke he'd been cradling

Because they'll never know I've been gone.

The boys who stopped by St Louis railroad station all had stories.

And they were anxious to tell them

Had I asked.

But reality is unknown

The truth too much to bear

Irreversible.

Books are safer . . .

Alice Story thinks I'm ready for some Sherwood Anderson.

Did Alice suspect? –

The book *Winesburg, Ohio* was published in 1919, two years after I was born.

He was a young and brilliant teacher. The boys at the school loved him; the townsfolk suspected him – of what they had not the language for, but whatever it was, it was different.

I had found what I was looking for . . .

Someone like me.

I may not be the only sissy in the world.

But how does it end?

(*Quoting.*) 'As he ran into the darkness, they ran after him, swearing and throwing sticks and great balls of soft mud at the figure that screamed and ran faster.'

How it always ends

Something or someone is heard in the wood – a shriek, a call – it could be a fox or a person.

Beat.

He wonders what it's about but carries on.

None of the railroad boys ever made fun out of me.

He breaks some ice and pours himself a drink.

I was never beaten up.

They recognised, I guess, that we were fellow aliens with no place to register.

Not then

Not before

Not now

> **Familiar Face** (*in a falsetto*)   How about letting me have this dance, sweetie?

And this guy – this *man* – was in his mid-forties, a father of five – a grandfather even – and a successful newspaper editor. Was he threatened by me? Offended? Challenged? A closet queen at heart?

No. That's too easy.

The homosexual problem –

Another shriek – **Merle** *ignores.*

> **George Weinberg**   'The homosexual problem'

George Weinberg, again

> **George Weinberg**   is the problem of condemning variety in human existence. If one cannot enjoy the fact of this variety, at the very least one must learn to become indifferent to it, since obviously it is here to stay.

The fear of it will not simply go away

Merle *takes a couple of pills, to take the edge off.*

And so what choice do we have then but to run?

The voices, the band – they start to settle down.

That's enough for today.

(*Calling.*) Lights out.

He goes around the room, turning all the lamps off. He takes the baseball bat from the shelf.

David, can you make sure the heater's on in the room?

David? Are you alive?

Hello?

All the lights are now off. He steps outside onto the verandah.

Silence.

The outside suddenly comes into focus for **Merle** *– the sounds of the night.*

Brilliant moon tonight.

And Venus is looking very bright

Or whatever that one is . . .

The shriek again – it's close; it's human.

He grips the baseball bat. He's frightened.

He looks back at the house.

(*Calling.*) David? David!

He sees his reflection – doubled, trebled, quadrupled in all the glass; the figure is frightened, his guard is up.

10. Sad Gay World

Morning. Snow blankets the house.

Merle *is outside, wrapped up against the cold.*

Merle   He's gone to get wood.

Keeping the talent alive . . .

It blew in from the east. Quite unannounced.

As was he

Strong, tall . . . untamed . . .

I know. I saddled myself with an alpha. All six foot three of him. A real Jack Armstrong.

Stick with a hunter/gatherer, people. You'll be just fine in an apocalypse.

Should that go in? Am I offering relationship advice now?

Before David it was Bill. This house was built for Bill. Bill – the suit salesman. Our prism in the pines.

And now it's David.

They say I thought it was a good relationship?

I say it is . . . but it's still a relationship.

And they're all the same, no matter the gender of the people involved. It's never easy. I've tried it three times on what I hoped would be a permanent basis. Once, the marriage, Elinor; the second, Bill – ten years; and the third . . .

We probably

Definitely

Drink too much.

But we understand one another. He's teaching me patience and I gave him teeth again. Crowned. We're slowly helping each other be . . .

Who we are.

And though I'm nearly twice his age I can't help thinking he's . . . carved out of something more solid . . .

I don't want to ruin this one.

Martin Hoffman   Self condemnation.

Martin Hoffman, the voice of reason again –

Martin Hoffman   Pervades the homosexual world and makes stable relationships a terrific problem.

Surely it's a problem for everyone.

Martin Hoffman   Lonely and alone, many can't seem to find someone with whom to share even a part of their lives.

I have found someone. I'm leaving this entire house – all twenty-six acres – to him!

Martin Hoffman   This dilemma –

He says he doesn't deserve it.

I say what – deserve to be happy, safe, secure? What's wrong with you?

He says this isn't his life.

Martin Hoffman   This dilemma –

I say he should know I'm going to die first. And can't he see I want him to be ok?

Can't he see?

He goes quiet.

I shout.

Pause.

Martin Hoffman   This dilemma is the core problem of the gay world and until we can change these ancient attitudes, many men – including some of our brothers, sons, friends, colleagues and children yet unborn – will live out their lives in the quiet desperation of the sad gay world.

A moment.

Merle *laughs.*

I can see it on my gravestone.

Sad gay world.

A pain shoots up in **Merle**'s *stomach.*

(*In pain, uncensored.*) Goddammit!

Merle *takes a couple of breaths.*

But it's not in me to change the force of ancient attitudes. To change what's written into law? That's for someone else. Someone who has let their hair grow long and has sixty or so years ahead of them. Someone who can go proudly into the next decade and beyond saying Gay is Good, Gay is Proud without fear, without shame, without this . . . sadness.

What it means to be a homosexual? Easy.

Don't do what I did.

A long moment. He reflects on all the places he went wrong.

(*Sudden.*) Period. Full stop. The end.

Sign it off, cash the cheque, please, I am done.

He goes and opens the sliding door.

That's it.

You are free to leave.

I'm sure you're all tired of my voice

I know I am –

exhausted.

. . .

Leave the room.

Think what you may.

Show's over.

He goes inside, closing the door behind him.

The play is over. The house lights come up.

And then

from the audience

Boy from Pittsburgh *stands up.*

11. Boy from Pittsburgh

Boy from Pittsburgh (*from the audience*)   You're a coward.

That's what I think

A coward.

A long moment.

Yeah, you – behind the door

Merle *opens the door.*

Merle   Is there a problem?

Boy from Pittsburgh   Nothing you can fix.

Merle   I knew someone was there –

Boy from Pittsburgh   Nothing you can make better.

Merle   I knew it –

Boy from Pittsburgh   I should've known.

Merle   Is someone having some kind of grievance?

Boy from Pittsburgh   A grievance? (*To the audience.*) This guy . . .

(*To* **Merle.**) I'm having a dilemma, how about that.

Merle   Ok, well I guess that's to be expected –

Boy from Pittsburgh   This is a waste of my time –

Merle   I can't see that far. Can someone – I – can you move into the light?

Boy from Pittsburgh   No – fuck you, man.

Merle   Excuse me?

Boy from Pittsburgh   I'm not here, I don't exist, don't panic – go back to your safe little world –

Merle (*to the audience*)   Well, this is exciting. I am at a total loss at what to do –

Boy from Pittsburgh   Stop that –

Merle   Stop what?

Boy from Pittsburgh   Stop brushing off everything as if it doesn't matter. You think this is funny?

Merle *looks around for help.*

Merle   I most certainly do not.

Boy from Pittsburgh   Then why you giving up?

Merle   I've reached the end.

Boy from Pittsburgh   But I don't like this end.

Merle   I can see this young man has something to say.

Boy from Pittsburgh   What?

Merle   You're standing up, you have our attention

Boy from Pittsburgh   I . . .

Merle   Speak.

Beat.

Boy from Pittsburgh *stays still.*

Merle   Alright, can someone bring him up? Anyone?

Boy from Pittsburgh *is escorted to the stage.*

Merle   The floor is yours.

Boy from Pittsburgh *is silent.*

Merle   This isn't the ending you want, you end it.

I'm sure you'll do a beautiful job.

Beat.

Boy from Pittsburgh (*quietly*)   Sad gay world.

Merle   You're going to have to speak up if you want to be / heard

Boy from Pittsburgh (*loud*)   Sad gay world?

'. . . many men will live out their lives in the quiet desperation of the sad gay world.'

Merle   So you're quoting my essay, ok . . .

Boy from Pittsburgh   And then what?

Merle   What do you mean?

Boy from Pittsburgh   What's the next sentence?

Merle   You seem to have very strong opinions, you tell me.

Boy from Pittsburgh   But you're the adult –

Merle   I'm just an old hack –

Boy from Pittsburgh   You're living it –

Merle   And I've given as much as I can

Boy from Pittsburgh   It's not good enough.

Merle   I am trying to do something very hard.

Boy from Pittsburgh   Are you serious?

Merle   And I would prefer you not to pick holes in a work-in-progress.

Boy from Pittsburgh   Look at you. Look at this.

What's so hard about this?

Merle   It's difficult to convey in an essay –

Boy from Pittsburgh   Your 'prism in the pines' . . . 'miles away from anywhere' . . . writing stories of what you think is real.

Merle   I haven't always lived this way.

And if you've been listening, you would have heard that.

Boy from Pittsburgh   The pain got too much though and you checked out.

Moved on. Ran.

Well, I can't hide yet. I'm in it, and there's no escape. There's no escaping . . .

Me.

And I can't see a future where I'm going to be ok – where it's ever going to be . . .

He puts his head in his hands.

Merle   Oh no, don't . . .

He looks offstage.

Can someone . . . anyone?

No?

He sees he's on his own.

Do you have a name?

Boy from Pittsburgh   I'm not giving you my name.

Merle   No sure – sure.

Have you come far?

Boy from Pittsburgh   Pittsburgh.

Merle   Well . . . hello, Pittsburgh.

I'm listening.

Boy from Pittsburgh   What's there to say? It's the same story.

As he ran into the darkness, they ran after him, swearing and throwing sticks . . .

Only I got caught.

Merle   The vice squad?

Boy from Pittsburgh   He offered me a ride. He was – I thought – he was interested . . . in me.

I'm an idiot.

Merle   No.

Boy from Pittsburgh   I was his 219th arrest. He enjoyed telling me that.

Merle   What an asshole.

And so were you . . .

Boy from Pittsburgh   Jail. And I've been kicked out of nursing school – without a hearing. My whole future gone. Any prospect of . . . because it's hard enough . . . it's been, always . . . and now – on my record forever.

And they're threatening to tell my mom. She's all I have left.

Merle   How old are you?

Boy from Pittsburgh   Seventeen.

Beat.

Merle   I'm sorry. That's too much for a young person.

Boy from Pittsburgh   Yeah, well . . . this is what you get when you're . . .

Because I'm –

Beat.

Merle   Have you tried the American Civil Liberties Union? Have you contacted them? I used to be on their board. I can ring them – they can help –

Boy from Pittsburgh   Like you helped?

Merle   It was a different time.

You should ring them.

Boy from Pittsburgh   No – if I do that my mom will hear about it and she'll kick me out and I'll be homeless –

Merle   No, look, it's important to stay rational.

Boy from Pittsburgh   I'm a pervert. That's what happens. We get kicked out. I'd do the same to me. Who wants a dirty fag for a son, right?

Merle   Please don't use language like that.

Boy from Pittsburgh   What do you care?

Merle   Would you at least be open to a conversation with her?

Boy from Pittsburgh   You don't get it.

Merle   She may already know.

Boy from Pittsburgh   No.

Merle   The things we spend our lives knowing and pretending not to know –

Boy from Pittsburgh   Stop!

Merle   I'm trying to help you here.

Boy from Pittsburgh   You've proved you can't – you're, you're old and scared and –

Merle   You should be thankful I'm offering you advice –

Boy from Pittsburgh   Thankful?

Merle   I had no one. None of us back then had anyone. None. We were scrambling in the dark and you're here – disrupting!

Boy from Pittsburgh   So that's your excuse for doing nothing?

Merle   I'm doing something now.

Boy from Pittsburgh   It's not enough. None of it is enough.

Merle   I can't do this.

He looks to the wings for help.

I'm sorry – can someone . . .

Boy from Pittsburgh   No, don't do that -

Merle   Please . . .

Boy from Pittsburgh *takes out a copy of* **Merle**'s *novel* What Happens.

Merle   What's that?

Boy from Pittsburgh   The one you're writing now.

Merle   My book? No – I would never approve that cover.

Boy from Pittsburgh   Why did you kill him?

Merle   . . .

Boy from Pittsburgh   George Lionel? The one who couldn't handle himself or the world around him and so (*mimes firing a gun*).

Merle   He's only fiction, kid.

Boy from Pittsburgh   And the answer's always the same: annihilation, because it would be too much to live. The future? Loveless, cold and alone. Just kill yourself.

What kind of an ending is that?

Merle   Well, if you're going to crudely simplify a three-year writing process –

Boy from Pittsburgh   What ending is that?

Merle   You know, there is a *journey* he goes on / I didn't just –

Boy from Pittsburgh   / I need you to give me one good reason why I shouldn't kill myself.

Beat.

Merle   Don't play games.

This isn't funny.

Boy from Pittsburgh   Now you're getting it.

One good reason.

Or I'm going to walk out of here, buy a gun and blow my brains out.

Happily.

Merle   Ok.

Boy from Pittsburgh   Ok?!

Merle   Do you want to give me a second here?

A moment, or two.

Ok. So your mom.

Boy from Pittsburgh   No –

Merle   Often things come back to mothers, fathers. It's irritating. Get over it.

Now what makes you think she won't be able to survive this?

Boy from Pittsburgh   I'm all she has.

Merle   Mothers are sturdier than you think. I mean, they've been hearing such information about their children for a long time now –

Boy from Pittsburgh   She's different.

Merle   And I know of no instance of one dying from shock.

The question is, can you handle yourself?

Beat.

And then **Boy from Pittsburgh** *starts to cry.*

Boy from Pittsburgh   I don't want her to die.

Merle   I know you don't. But the thing is, I don't want you to die.

I really don't.

A moment.

Sugar.

Do not move.

If you will insist on standing out in the cold.

He gets up. He goes inside and gets some coffee and cheesecake.

Boy from Pittsburgh *sits alone on stage, trying to staunch the tears.*

Merle *returns with the cheesecake.*

Merle (*light*)   Ok, just try it. Because it goes well with the coffee. And David made it – he's a superb baker.

He serves it.

It's the graham crackers that makes the crumb.

Boy from Pittsburgh *takes a bite.*

Merle   Not bad?

Boy from Pittsburgh   I mean – it's cheesecake.

Merle (*laughing*)   It is.

Another reason to avoid suicide? You're young. You don't get that now. But if you ended it you would miss out on the gay revolution. And revolutions are always fun – especially if they're bloodless.

Boy from Pittsburgh   I don't want to fight though.

Merle   I don't think we have a choice.

You know, there may be a time when words like homosexual will disappear from the human language, but that hasn't happened yet, and in the meantime we are in trouble for who we are.

Until that fact is faced, until people have the guts to say what they are – to live how they are . . . nothing will change.

A moment.

I attended an anniversary party the other day. Two of our kind and . . . they've been together for twenty-five years.

It's true.

It gives me hope.

Boy from Pittsburgh   Are they happy?

Merle   Reasonably. They still hold hands – though not in public. And they are kind to each other, which is rare anywhere these days, right?

A moment.

Boy from Pittsburgh *relaxes a bit.*

Merle   I am sorry about George. But that's not how it ends.

Boy from Pittsburgh   Did I read it wrong?

Merle   No. You didn't.

Beat.

Merle   Do you need rest?

Boy from Pittsburgh *shakes his head.*

Merle   I think you need rest.

Boy from Pittsburgh *lies down on the verandah.*

Boy from Pittsburgh   Can you stay with me? Just for a minute.

Merle   I stayed with him.

I don't know if I was any help – if I convinced him not to, but I felt I had a shot at . . . at the other thing.

And so I laid down my self-pity and wariness and I . . . I . . .

He goes back inside to the typewriter and starts typing.

12. What It No Longer Need Mean

January 1971.

Merle *is on* The Dick Cavett Show.

Bright studio lights, audience applause – lots of smiles.

> **Merle**   What was the question?
>
> Oh, that's right.
>
> Should a writer reveal that much of himself.
>
> *A moment.*
>
> I've always thought that one of the obligations of a writer is to expose as much of themselves as possible. To be as open and honest as they can manage. So that their readers can see in what they write a reflection of themselves – weaknesses and strengths, courage and cowardice, good and evil.
>
> Isn't that one of the reasons writing is perhaps the most painful of the arts?

Merle *smiles for approval from beyond. The lights go down.*

Back in the Glass House.

> **Victor**   Merle, it's beautiful. We're running it.
>
> **Merle**   Victor, are you sure? You don't want to think about it a bit more? Maybe a few cuts? The railroad bit . . .?
>
> **Victor**   No – no cuts – it's perfect – it's going to be –
>
> **Merle**   Their lead piece, Elinor. Over-egging a bit don't you think?
>
> **Elinor**   Wait – I'm nearly done . . .
>
> *A moment as the draft is proofread again.*
>
> **Elinor**   'What It Means to Be a Homosexual' . . .

> **Merle**   Victor's title.
>
> **Elinor**   You can't get more direct than that, can you.
>
> **Merle**   I hope you're not upset by it.
>
> **Elinor**   Oh, Merle. Would it matter if I was?

I stay in the house.

And wait.

Outside, the world celebrates in 1971. Fireworks. Inside, Merle watches them explode around him.

Weeks go by.

> **Victor**   We got a photographer coming down to yours tomorrow. Nothing fancy. Just you in a few turtlenecks, looking . . . looking good.

At least Mother was nearly blind.

Camera flashes. **Merle** *is trying to find the right pose.*

Hundreds of photos are being taken.

Over nine hundred.

That's got to be it, no?

> **Photographer**   We'll get there.

Try looking proud.

Right down the lens.

Still.

Merle   Too fey.

Too sissy.

Too –

> **Photographer**   Eyes up.
>
> **Merle**   I think you've got it.

The flashing comes to an end.

But how different my life would have been if I'd been born in 1950 instead of . . .

No.

Stop it.

That's a tiresome game, and I'm too old to play it.

No one's going to *read* it anyway. They'll skim over. I don't know what I'm expecting

At least now I can finally finish the novel.

What's the date again?

I am suggested to be on the David Frost Show to discuss the subject. Only to be told by the producer that I was 'unacceptable'.

Why?

'Because we are a family programme'

I stay in the house.

I run out of milk.

David's away.

Oh hell.

He wraps himself up – scarf, sunglasses and all.

The effort to go was equivalent to the first island landing on the Pacific in the spring of '45.

In the store –

I have a nodding acquaintance with almost everybody. And while no West 42nd Street, I was pretty sure of the liberalness of the town.

I enter the store.

So far so clear.

I get to the counter –

Lord in heaven.

Father Daniel is serving me.

At this point I'm readying myself to be taken out and stoned.

But then –

Father Daniel reaches out and says

> **Father Daniel**   I want to shake your hand. That was a
> very important piece you wrote, and I'm glad you did
> it. We need to get these things out in the open and
> discuss them.

I keep forgetting.

And I mustn't.

The basic of decency of people.

And to think it took me almost fifty years to come out of the
closet, to stop pretending I was something I wasn't, most of
the time fooling nobody, to receive . . .

Boy from Pittsburgh *comes in with a sack of letters.*

Merle   Letters explaining if they come out, doctors and
therapists would lose their patients, lawyers would lose their
practices; writers would lose their readers, teachers their
positions . . .

What can I say?

Each person must come out at their own time, and in their
own way. But all have an obligation to declare themselves
whenever we decently can. No minority has gained its rights
by remaining silent, and no revolution has ever been made
by the wary.

Or the self-pitying.

Over two thousand.

A record high for the magazine.

What does that mean?

One from a girl who now edits my old paper, *The Daily Iowan* –

Oh God. The young.

Boy from Pittsburgh (*reading*)   'Articles such as yours make it easier for all persons who deviate from the norm – read white, straight, middle-class, Protestant male. We understand that all oppression is interrelated: that the treatment accorded people of colour, women, gay people all derives from the same source, that until we are free, none will be free . . . I think you would have felt more comfortable working for this year's staff, but we still have a long way to go.'

Merle   I love the young! Always have. I have never been one of those who are threatened by the young.

Boy from Pittsburgh *takes out another letter.*

Boy from Pittsburgh (*reading*)   'Everyone is misjudged and misunderstood on occasion, but the shame of our society that we should tolerate discrimination against homosexuals is deplorable, and I cringe to realise I've been even a small part of it!'

Merle   Given a chance, most people are basically decent.

Boy from Pittsburgh (*reading*)   'I feel confident that others are gaining a healthier attitude toward this long-existing problem and, hopefully, the present generation will prove wiser than its often close-minded and narrow-thinking elders.'

The phone rings.

> **Mother**   (*Sighs.*)
>
> **Merle**   Hello, Mother.
>
> **Mother**   We're wiping you out of our will.

Merle   But you always told me to tell the truth.

Mother   I know but not that kind of truth.

Merle *sifts through the letters.*

I sometimes wonder what would happen if we announced it all at once, every one of us – the obscure and the famous and all those in between . . . it would create a quiet revolution – all by itself it would.

Boy from Pittsburgh *hands* **Merle** *a letter to read.*

Merle (*reading*)   'Your article – while totally honest for you – was not true for us. This isn't a put-down. It's to say that from where we stand, some things are clear in our lives that can't be part of your experience. For us this was not 'what it means to be a homosexual', but what it no longer need mean.

Pause.

What it no longer need mean . . .

Perhaps I should have called it that.

13. The Glass House

Sunday 28 June 1971.

Merle *opens the door to the outside to let the breeze in.*

Merle   I realise how stifling the air has been all these years. I may not be freer, but I'm a lot more comfortable, a lot less cramped.

He gets ready to leave.

I'm going to the city.

There's a march.

The second Christopher Street March. I'm not missing it. We need the numbers. People listen to numbers. And then after that to Washington, DC for the first gay rally there – in front of the White House would you believe.

Yes, I'm an activist now – touring all over the country giving talks to anyone else who'll listen. And when someone asks me about the article, I always say the same thing.

> **Merle**   I don't think what I did was particularly courageous. But what I do think is if you can relieve the guilt of ten people in your lifetime . . . well, then, I think you've made a contribution.

His typewriter goes.

My final crusade.

The house starts to disappear.

There are some things that are going to happen that I hate. When I die – not planned, my stomach, it's always my stomach – they won't mention David.

The New York Times obituary will be sad in tone and, well, just sad really. David, my love for over twenty years, deleted. My close friends, deleted.

The house is almost gone.

It will be a solitary sketch of a man, a long way from the flesh and blood truth.

He is left alone on an empty stage.

And those who caused a lot of pain for my community will outlive me. They will thrive and work and maybe never really understand.

The light starts to darken.

I don't know if I said what I needed to have said.

Whether any of it was right.

But I do know

That this house will be gone

My prism in the pines gone

And all the voices

The faces

Gone.

But today

Oh, today the air is extraordinary clear.

And I would not choose to be –

Blackout.

End of play.

www.ingramcontent.com/pod-product-compliance
Ingram Content Group UK Ltd.
Pitfield, Milton Keynes, MK11 3LW, UK
UKHW020709280225
455688UK00012B/330

9 781350 425163